THE COZY BOOK

THE

ILLUSTRATED BY BETTY FRASER

MARY ANN HOBERMAN

BROWNDEER PRESS
HARCOURT BRACE & COMPANY
San Diego   New York   London

FOR
THREE SMALL COUSINS
EMILY FREEDMAN
REBECCA IAFRATI
LUCIE LEDBETTER
M.A.H.

Requests for permission to make copies of any part of the work should be
mailed to: Permissions Department, Harcourt Brace & Company,
6277 Sea Harbor Drive, Orlando, Florida 32887-6777.

Browndeer Press is a registered trademark of Harcourt Brace & Company.

Library of Congress Cataloging-in-Publication Data
Hoberman, Mary Ann.
The cozy book/Mary Ann Hoberman; illustrated by Betty Fraser.
p.   cm.
"Browndeer Press."
Summary: Verses describe a variety of foods, activities, smells, sounds, words,
places, people, feelings, and other things perceived as being cozy.
ISBN 0-15-276620-0
1. Children's poetry, American. [1. American poetry.]
I. Fraser, Betty, ill. II. Title.
PS3558.O3367C6   1995
811'.54—dc20   93-10826

First edition
A B C D E
Printed in Singapore

The paintings in this book were done in Winsor & Newton gouache and
  watercolor on bristol paper.
The display and text type were set in Berkeley Old Style by
  Harcourt Brace & Company Photocomposition Center, San Diego, California.
Color separations were made by Bright Arts, Ltd., Singapore.
Printed and bound by Tien Wah Press, Singapore
This book was printed with soya-based inks on Leykam recycled paper, which
  contains more than 20 percent postconsumer waste and has a total recycled
  content of at least 50 percent.
Production supervision by Warren Wallerstein and Diana Ford
Designed by Linda Lockowitz

When you wake up bright and early
In your roasty toasty bed
With your covers wrapped around you
And your pillow on your head
And you peek out at the morning
That's a cozy kind of way
To begin the cozy doings
Of a very cozy day.

You get up a little later
And you put some cozy clothes on—
Shirt and sweater, corduroys—
And after you have those on
It is time to eat your breakfast
So you sit down in your seat—
Later on come lunch and supper—
All the cozy things to eat!

Scrambled eggs stirred soft and sunny
Melted cheese that's nice and runny
Fresh-baked muffins dripping honey
Chocolate pudding, bread and butter
Fluffy mounds of mashed potatoes

Jelly doughnuts, milk and cookies
Toast and tea when you are sick
Applesauce strained smooth and thick
(Lumpy food is never cozy)

Juicy peaches fat and fuzzy
Sliced bananas, tapioca—
Sliced bananas? Tapioca?
Well, certain people think they're cozy—
You may not
Some don't
Some do
What you like is up to you
(But everyone thinks cocoa's cozy)
Whipped-up frothy orange Jell-O
Chicken soup with spots of yellow
Creamed tomato red and rosy—
Cozy cozy cozy cozy.

Afterwards you go and play
What are cozy things to do?

Pat-a-cake and one potato
Piggyback and peekaboo
Cozy games that last all morning
House and store and school and doctor
Setting up your tracks and trains
Getting out your boats and planes
Making roads for cars and trucks
Building towns with blocks and bricks

If it's nice, you go outside—
Sandbox, seesaw, swing and slide—
All the cozy games to play
Which ones will you choose today?

Flying kites and jumping rope

Tag and hopscotch, hide-and-seek

Bouncing balls and blowing bubbles   Blindman's buff (but do not peek!)

Dig a hole straight down to China
Build a castle in the sand
Hide inside a weeping willow

Plant a garden
Start a stand

Make-believe and let's pretend
Tell a secret to a friend

Sing a-ring-around-the-rosy—
Cozy cozy cozy cozy.

Sniff the air for cozy smells:
Smell of flowers, fire, food
Roses blooming
Wood that's burning
Bread that's baking
They smell good!

Fresh-dug earth
New-mown hay
New-cut grass
New-born day
Washing drying on the line—
That smells fine!

Popcorn that has just been popped
Kitchen floor that's just been mopped
Onions that have just been chopped
Stop your crying!
Smell them frying!

Some smells make you think of things
Things you think you had forgot
If a smell helps you remember
Call it a forget-me-not

Places that you like smell cozy
People that you love smell cozy
You do, too—
To you, you do!
(How to tell a smell is cozy?
You won't know unless you're nosy!)

I am nosy

Cock your ear for cozy sounds:

Bird cheep

Mouse peep

Bug buzz

Brook burble

Bee bumble

Baby babble

Lip smacking

Toe tapping

Cheek popping

Hand clapping

Tongue clicking

Clock ticking

Wood chopping

Wave lapping

Straw sipping

Rain dripping

Fan whirring

Cat purring

Chick cluck
Duck quack
Goose honk
Pig oink

Sheep baa
Horse neigh
Cow moo
Cock crow

Mud squish   Snowcrust crunch   Snap of dry leaf underfoot

The gurgle that a gargle makes
The giggle when a tickle takes

Hurdy-gurdy
Music box
Bells that jingle ting-a-ling
Piano tinkle
Pipe of flute
A little strum upon a string
A little tune you like to hum
A little song you like to sing
A little whistle on your lips—
Music is a cozy thing.

Traffic rumble
Airplane roar
Freight train toot
Grandpa's snore
All sound cozy
From afar

Laughs and chuckles   Squeaky kisses   Whispers, murmurs, lullabies—

Hush and listen!   Close your eyes!

What sounds cozy through and through?
Say it softly—

I love you

Words are cozy

Mumble
Scribble
Sandal
Muzzle

Alabama

Cuspidor and Orphan Annie

Pachysandra
Sarsaparilla
Tusk and smug and fog
Galoshes

Ambidextrous
Henrietta

Cozy places?
Attics, cellars
Closets, cupboards
Nooks and crannies
Halfway up or down the stair
Underneath a chair or table
Tucked behind a screen or curtain.

Cozy places?
Alleys, tunnels
Caves and secret passages
Tent and treehouse
Clubhouse, haystack
Hideaway in rocky hollow
Places that are hushed and hidden
Spaces that are dark and warm

Go and find your teddy bear
Snuggle underneath your blanket
Cover up from top to toesy—
Cozy cozy cozy cozy.

People can be cozy, too
People that you like to be with
And that like to be with you

People who can understand you

People who will hear your troubles

People who will keep your secrets

People who have pleasant voices

People who have happy smiles

People who know how to listen

Like to play, tell jokes and stories
Like to help you, like to *like* you
Like to laugh, but not at you

Sometimes they are skinny thinny

Sometimes they are roly-poly

Sometimes short and sometimes tall

Sometimes young and sometimes old

Sometimes he and sometimes she
But whatever they may be
They are always nice to be with
Nice to stay with
Spend the day with

Laps to sit in, hands to hold
Arms to hug you when you're cold
Lips to kiss you, soft and rosy—
Cozy cozy cozy cozy.

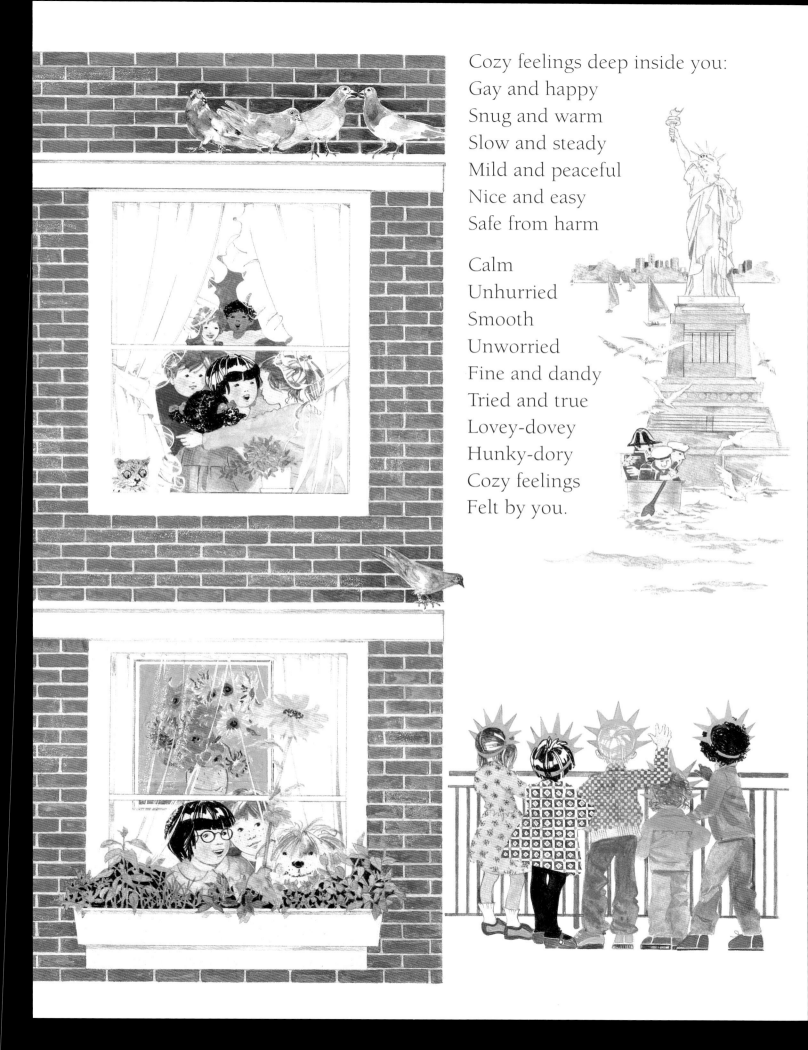

Cozy feelings deep inside you:
Gay and happy
Snug and warm
Slow and steady
Mild and peaceful
Nice and easy
Safe from harm

Calm
Unhurried
Smooth
Unworried
Fine and dandy
Tried and true
Lovey-dovey
Hunky-dory
Cozy feelings
Felt by you.

Other kinds of cozy feelings
Things to feel that feel so nice:

Petting puppies   Patting mudpies

Finger painting   Sucking ice

Lick a lolly

Blow a candle

Pick a posy

Hold a hand

Catch a snowflake on your tongue

Scrunch your toe into the sand

Whittle down a stick of softwood   Kick a pebble on a path

Squish into a squashy cushion   Sink into a brimming bath

Back rubs, bear hugs, cuddles, squeezes
Sneezing long-awaited sneezes
Laughing till you're all in stitches
Scratching in the place it itches
Whiskers (when they're not too prickly)
Tickles (when they're not too tickly)

Gliding in a squeaky glider
Rocking in a rocking chair
Swaying in a swaying hammock—
Cozy feelings everywhere.

Cozy things we haven't named yet?

Turkey stuffing
Rabbit tail

Turtle
Thimble
Birthday presents
English sheepdogs
Ginger ale

Lucky pennies
Circus ponies
Macaroni
Curly hair

Cradles
Dimples
Apple dumplings
Cotton candy
Solitaire

Hot fudge sundaes
No-school Mondays
Picture postcards
Matching twins

Unbaked batter
Butter fingers
Monkey business
Safety pins

Four-leaf clover
Yankee Doodle
Jack-o'-lantern
Sugarplum

Chocolate kisses
Spring vacation
Hibernation
Bubble gum

Shiny lockets
Zipper pockets
Easter bunny
Honeycomb

Wells for wishing
Going fishing
Going barefoot
Going home.

And now the cozy day is gone
And now the cozy book is read

Of all the cozy things there are
The coziest of all is bed.

So go to sleep, sweet sleepyhead

Just curl up snug and shut the light

A good-night hug, a kiss good-night

Sweet thoughts
Sweet dreams
Sleep deep
Sleep tight

Droopy
Drifty
Drowsy Dozy—

Dream of everything that's cozy.